A. B. von Landsberg

The Green Vaults Dresden

Illustrations of the choicest works in that museum of art

A. B. von Landsberg

The Green Vaults Dresden
Illustrations of the choicest works in that museum of art

ISBN/EAN: 9783743608528

Printed in Europe, USA, Canada, Australia, Japan

Cover: Foto ©Thomas Meinert / pixelio.de

Manufactured and distributed by brebook publishing software (www.brebook.com)

A. B. von Landsberg

The Green Vaults Dresden

Johann Melchior Dinglinger

THE GREEN VAULTS

DRESDEN.

ILLUSTRATIONS OF THE CHOICEST WORKS

IN THAT

MUSEUM OF ART.

EXECUTED IN LITHOCROMY BY STORCH AND KRAMER FROM DRAWINGS BY SEIDEMANN AND MOHN.
WITH DESCRIPTIONS BY MAJOR BARON VON LANDSBERG AND ALEXANDER ALLEN ESQ.

EDITED BY

LEWIS GRUNER

AUTHOR OF ILLUSTRATIONS OF "FRESCO DECORATIONS" "SPECIMENS OF ORNAMENTAL ART" "SCULPTURES OF ORVIETO CATHEDRAL" &c.
AND OF "CAPELLA CHIGIANA" "H. M. PAVILION IN THE GARDENS OF BUCKINGHAM PALACE" AND OTHER SIMILAR WORKS

DRESDEN
C. C. MEINHOLD AND SONS
1862.

The wish has often been expressed in past times by students and lovers of art to possess faithful representations of the most important, and interesting objects in the celebrated collection of the *"Green Vaults"* at Dresden.

A mere hurried inspection of treasures so varied, multitudinous, and instructive was felt to be insufficient and unsatisfactory by those who were aware, that artistic taste finds its expression not only in architecture, sculpture, and painting, but likewise in many articles destined merely for domestic use or ornament; and who therefore, recognized the importance of this collection to the history of art, to the artist, and even to the artizan. It would be useless to specify here the difficulties, which, till now, have prevented the gratification of this desire. The love and knowledge of art, which, in earlier times, was confined to the student and the amateur, may be said in a certain sense to have extended itself in our days to the whole of the educated public. We see even the manufacturer and the handicraftsman eagerly on the look-out for beautiful models and designs for their productions, and an increased love and appreciation of artistic merit on the part of the purchaser. It may therefore without impropriety be said, that, what was formerly the wish of the few has become the want of the many.

With permission of his gracious majesty the King of Saxony, a selection, as a beginning, has now been made of some of the most striking objects of this rich collection; photographs have been taken of them, these carefully copied on stone and reproduced by the aid of Chromolithography with a success, it is believed, hitherto unsurpassed. The result is offered to the public in the accompanying illustrations.

A short sketch will not be here out of place of the origin, history, and nature of the Collection from which these specimens have been selected. Among the nations of Antiquity, it was the practice to preserve and guard, with almost religious veneration and care, in localities especially appropriated to the purpose, and called "Treasuries", family valuables, trophies, national memorials, and the like. This custom was continued among modern nations, and almost every court possessed its Treasury, which was more or less rich. Its contents were in a state of continual increase: in it were deposited the offerings of friendship and of love, memorials of important family or national events, the rarest valuables, bridal gifts, votive offerings, reliquaries, church plate, etc. etc.

We must keep in mind that these articles were, as a rule, the most costly, remarkable, and beautiful, which the taste of the day could discover, its best art produce, or which were rendered interesting by personal or historical associations. If many of them cannot be regarded strictly as works of art, we must remember that, at the time of their acquisition, they were objects of curiosity, either on account of their rarity, or the difficulty of their execution; and judge them by the taste and cultivation of their period. Like all the ruling families, the Saxon Princes also possessed their treasures. From the earliest times of which we have notice they were located in a couple of strong vaulted chambers, called The *"Green Vaults"*, on the ground floor of the palace at Dresden. A secret passage was said to lead from these to the dwelling of the Ruler, and it was believed that none but he and his confidants could enter them. Be that as it may, their contents were guarded and preserved with jealous care, and some degree of mystery; and in consequence, at one time, were held to be of fabulous value by the vulgar.

Much trifling controversy has taken place as to the origin of the epithet *"green"*; some attributing it to the colour of earlier decorations of the chambers themselves (of which, however no record is preserved), some to the fact of a door having led from them into a shrubbery, which formerly lay between them and an ancient gate of the city called the *"Green Gate"*; while others, with more probability, have found its explanation in the Green of the plant *Rue*, which appears in the arms, or is the badge of the House of Saxony. In the time of the Elector Augustus the First (his beneficent rule extends from 1553 to 1586) this rudimentary collection received considerable additions. This enlightened monarch seems to have been a man considerably in advance of his times. He founded in the upper floor of his palace a "Cabinet of Art and Curiosities" in connection with and supplementary to the hereditary and personal treasures of the *"Green Vaults"*. In it were preserved mechanical, mathematical, and surgical instruments, minerals, books, pictures, watches, natural curiosities, and artistic rarities of various kinds. He seems to have been influenced less by the pleasure of collecting than by a patriotic desire for the improvement of his people. His acquisitions were intended for the benefit of the public, as examples of what sagacity, reflection, and patient toil had produced elsewhere of beautiful and useful in the circle of the Arts and Sciences, as a spur to the diligence and an incentive to the imitative powers of his people. In this collection we may see the cradle of many of the rich and valuable ones, which form at the present day the pride and boast of the Saxon capital. His more immediate successors from generation to generation continued to add to these treasures in the same spirit. Large additions were made to them by Augustus the Second, commonly called "The Strong", Elector of Saxony and King of Poland (reigned from 1697 — 1733). Soon after his accession, a fire broke out in his palace in the immediate vicinity of the "Cabinet of Art and Curiosities", which rendered the immediate removal of its contents necessary. The most valuable articles were hastily stored away in some fireproof chambers of the ground floor, where they remained in great confusion for many years. The invasion of the Swedes under Charles XII, the king's own campaigns in Poland, and his frequent journeys thither, long prevented any steps being taken for their arrangement. Upon the coming of more peaceful times, this magnificent-spirited and splendour-loving Monarch caused the family accumulations in art and science and their treasures of all kinds, to be carefully examined, and systematically arranged. What more strictly belonged to pure art or science was consigned to their respective departments; a new "Cabinet of Curiosities" was founded to receive those articles which, according to our mode of viewing them, were remarkable rather for handicraft or rarity than for artistic worth, and the remaining costly, valuable, and rare treasures were incorporated with those of the *"Green Vaults"*, room being made for them by the addition of several adjoining chambers. The whole was decorated with great magnificence at the private expense of the king, and under his personal superintendence. The collection was indebted to his munificence for many costly additions, and remained the object of his fond care and attention up to the period of his death. With the exception of his immediate successor, none of the subsequent Saxon rulers have contributed much to its increase. In 1769 some valuable acquisitions were made at a trifling cost at the sale of Count Bruehl's effects. From this time forward the troubles of war and higher and graver cares have occupied the minds of the Saxon monarchs, and no expenditure has been made on this collection, except what was necessary for its preservation and exhibition to the public, to whom it has been accessible under certain unavoidable restrictions from the time of Augustus the Strong. Since 1832 its contents have by degrees been re-arranged, so as to suit modern requirements and convenience: they are displayed in eight spacious chambers which remain unaltered, with their ancient and gorgeous decorations of marbles, mirrors, and now somewhat faded arabesques, as in the days of Augustus the Strong. The spectator is at first dazzled by the splendour, variety, and multitude of the objects which meet his view. He feels himself transported to a time, having no foreboding of the mournful earnestness of the present, when the world, amid its inevitable cares and toils, enjoyed with a simple and hearty appreciation those ingenious, magnificent, or beautiful objects, by which Art or patient toil sought to immortalize themselves. The Antiquarian will seek in vain in this collection gratification for his taste: with but few exceptions, the articles constituting it date from the beginning of the 16th till the middle of the 18th century. The Man of Taste, on the other hand, upon a minuter inspection, will find much that is beautiful in itself, much that is extraordinary in conception, rare in material, or of elaborate beauty of detail in execution. A brief enumeration of the nature of the articles constituting this, in its kind, unrivalled collection is all that our limited space allows. It contains bronzes, carvings in ivory, wood, amber, coral, wax, alabaster and soap stone, engraved shells, gems, cups and other vessels of half precious stones and rock crystal, mosaics, ancient and modern enamels, works in Niello, a great variety of embossed and incised metal work, gold, silver and gilt plate, richly adorned weapons, antique jewellery and trinkets, an immense collection of the rarest and most valuable precious stones, specimens of the mineral productions of Saxony, and finally a number of historical and miscellaneous toys, trinkets and natural curiosities.

The objects which have been selected for representation, belong, as may be gathered from the preceding, neither to ancient nor modern art, but to the so called Renaissance and Rococo period. It is hoped that the fidelity and beauty of execution of these plates may be thought not unworthy of the originals themselves, and of the collection from which they are taken.

April 1862.   A. A.

I.

Tankard or drinking Cup in carved ivory, mounted in silver gilt. Flemish.

Height 11¼ in.   Diameter 5¹⁄₂ in.

— — —.

This beautiful Tankard is a masterly production of the Flemish school, probably dating from the end of the 16th century. A triumphal procession of Neptune and Amphitrite is admirably carved in relief upon the body of the vessel. The lid is formed by a gracefully arranged, and carefully executed group of children, at play with dolphins and marine monsters. The mounting is of silver gilt, but without artistic merit. Like most of the specimens in this rich department of the collection, consisting of more than five hundred articles, this beautiful work is without the name or monogram of the artist.

II.

Model of a Dutch Frigate of ancient form, in ivory.

Height 3 f. 10 ⁀₂ in. Length 2 f. 9⅛ in.

This model, on account of its great size, could only be represented on a very reduced scale and without its stand. The latter is included, however, in the dimensions given above. It is one of the oldest specimens of the collection, regarded as a great curiosity, and still much admired. With the exception of the anchor, guns, and rigging, which are of gold, every part of the vessel and stand is of ivory. The main-sail displays the complete coat of arms of the House of Saxony, very delicately carved, and upon the hull between the planks, but not discernible in the plate without the aid of a glass, is to be found the genealogy of the Saxon rulers from Wittikind to the Elector John George I. .. The stand represents Neptune, in a shell-shaped chariot drawn by sea horses, and surrounded by marine divinities. This group, typical of the wild tempestuous element, is spirited, and of very creditable execution. The whole is the work of a much esteemed Flemish Artist, *Jacob Zeller*, settled at Deutz, near Cologne: it was completed in the year 1620.

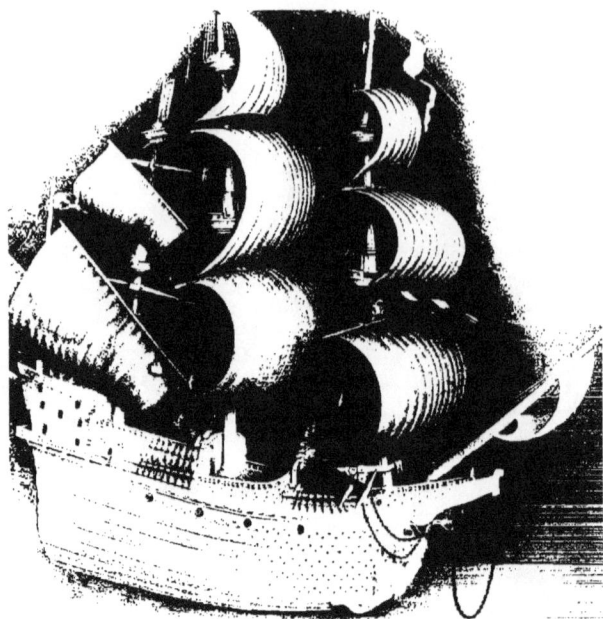

III.

An Indian Toilet Coffret, borne by an Elephant.

Height $5\frac{7}{12}$ in.   Length $7\frac{5}{12}$ in.

- - - -

This toilet-table decoration, which is of good workmanship, was brought by Augsburg traders to the fair at Leipsic, where it was purchased in 1731. Nothing further is known of its origin. Articles of a similar kind were executed in Delhi and Agra, as well as in China, and we trace something of an oriental character in this specimen. The trappings of the elephant are of gold and adorned with precious stones. The Coffret has the form of a building, with towers in the angles, and contains scent bottles and other small vessels in rock crystal mounted in gold.

IV.

A Nef in ivory.

Height 11¼ in. Length 9¼ in. Breadth 1⅛ in.

———————

Nothing is known of the history of this beautiful *Nef*. From the correct drawing, and graceful design, it has been attributed to a master of the 18ᵗʰ century. Another example, very similar in workmanship, exists in the collection, marked with the monogram "m: Ross: Zaïïï" which is not to be found in any dictionary of monograms. Upon the sides of the boat-shaped bowl, dolphins and sea-horses are carved in relief. The stem is formed by a figure of Neptune with his foot upon the head of a dolphin. A sea-horse surmounts the lid. *Nefs* were a favourite form for articles of table-decoration from the earliest times. They served among many other purposes for holding a napkin, which was at one time a luxury and distinction, accorded only to the guest of highest rank at the table. Our specimen was probably intended to contain incense, or other perfume for burning. Similar ones were occasionally used in the service of the mass.

V.

Nautilus Shell, mounted as a Drinking Cup.

Height 13 in. Breadth 8 in.

On the coast of Syria, and elsewhere in the East, nautilus, and other similarly formed shells were formerly, and may be still, in common use as drinking vessels. Many specimens of these primitive cups were brought to Europe by returning crusaders as objects of curiosity, or from some religious sentiment, or association, and afterwards preserved with almost reverential care among the family treasures of their descendants. At a later period many of these were again applied to their original destination, and mounted in the most costly manner, and in the most singular forms; perhaps, more as articles of display than of use. The collection contains upwards of one hundred specimens; most of which have been in the possession of the House of Saxony from a very early period. The present example is one of the most interesting among them, and is much admired by connoisseurs for the simple beauty of its form, and the excellence of its workmanship.

The shell is borne upon the shoulders of the sitting figure of a satyr, and upheld by its outstretched arms. A panther, which serves as a handle, surmounts the cup, the lip or mouth of which is formed by a grotesque mask of a silvan divinity, surrounded by elegantly designed foliage. This beautiful mounting is richly gilt, and is marked with the monogram "*B. O.*" and a small lion.

VI.

Nautilus Shell, mounted as a Drinking Vessel.

Height 19¼ in. Breadth 10½ in.

It requires but a superficial glance at this thoroughly fantastic creation, to feel embarrassed as to what time and style it is to be attributed. The shell itself is covered with a singular arabesque design in relief, with whimsical but highly original figures of delicate execution, etched in black at various points in the ground. The foot is formed by a silver-gilt monster like a dragon with eyes of garnet, terminating behind in a spray of coral, and carrying a figure in singular armour, with legs like the tail of a fish, and a tortoise for a saddle, which, with outstretched arms, bears aloft the shell. Another dragon-like monster silver-gilt, surmounts the whole, and forms a finish to the extremely tasteful mounting of the shell. It is not to be denied that this strange design produces an harmonious effect; and presents an interesting riddle, the solution of which is wanting. Neither monogram nor other mark exists on this piece to assist in determining its origin.

VII.

A. Nautilus Shell, mounted as a Cup or Drinking Vessel.

Height 7 ¼ in. Breadth 3⅔ in.

B. Small Ewer of Jasper.

–

The silver-gilt mounting of the shell, in the first specimen in the plate, is set with precious stones of considerable size, and terminates above in a grotesque head with an ape sitting upon it, which serves as a handle for the cup. The foot is formed by the trunk of a tree, and the figure of a woodman, who is represented as raising his axe with the purpose of cutting it down. Surrounding these is a sort of fence of silver basket work, encircled by an ornamental border, into which six small sea shells are introduced.

The design of this article displays more taste than that of most of the mounted shells in the collection; but the name of the artist, and the date of its execution have not been discovered.

The beautiful mounting of the second specimen is the work of Melchior Dinglinger.

VIII.

Gilt Ewer ornamented with oval Plaques or Panels of Mother of Pearl.

Height 14⅛ in. Diameter 4⅜ in.

This beautiful Ewer, belonging to a Plateau, or Basin of similar materials, is remarkable for its noble antique form. The embossed heads, and other ornaments are of very admirable workmanship; and the handle, especially, deserves attention for the elegance of its design, and its careful execution. All attempts, however, to discover the name of the artist, have proved unsuccessful.

IX.

Ewer of mother of pearl, mounted in silver gilt.

Height 12¼ in. Circumference 8⅝ in.

It is extremely to be regretted, that but few records have been preserved as to the makers' names, dates, and other interesting particulars relative to the numerous objects, forming the department of the collection from which the accompanying specimen is selected. With the exception of notices relating to their material worth, and the like, scarcely any written documents concerning them are in existence; most of the articles are without monogram or mark to aid in determining their origin and history. This beautiful ewer, with a plateau or stand of similar workmanship and material, has been among the treasures of the Green Vaults since the year 1640, and may be attributed, with tolerable certainty, from the beauty of the design and workmanship, to the best period of the silversmith's art. It was probably executed either at Nuremberg or Augsburg. From the twelfth century onwards, a rich collection of plate, and of costly vessels in gold, silver, and other materials was regarded as forming a necessary part of the splendour of every court, and was to be found more or less in all households of distinction. At banquets these articles were used to adorn the table, or were displayed upon buffets or moveable cupboards, generally placed near the host. Likewise, a number of these plateaus with ewers, filled with rosewater (at that time a rare and highly prized perfume) were placed either in the room itself, or in an adjoining one, for the use of the guests before sitting down to table, or for presentation to them, during, or at the close of the meal. It is supposed that it was the custom to pour a small quantity of the scented water over the fingers, a practice derived from the East, where it still prevails, and which found its way, by means of the Crusaders, through the Byzantine Empire and the Russian Principalities to the rest of Europe.

X.

A small Flask or Bottle, silver gilt, in the form of a Partridge.

During the middle ages, a taste for singularity of form in the vessels intended for table use or ornament, and for the decoration of the buffet, was universal in Germany; but it was not confined to that country. It is related, that, at the installation of the first Patriarch of Moscow in 1588, an incredible number of utensils in gold, large and small, in the forms of lions, elephants, bears, wolves, stags, hares, pelicans, owls, vultures, pheasants, partridges etc. etc. were displayed; and a considerable collection of such articles is still preserved in the Kremlin at Moscow. A like taste prevailed at the same period in France, and Italy; and we read, that at the opening of the tomb of the wife of the Emperor Honorius at Rome, in 1564, several articles of a similar kind were found, which would seem to indicate, that this passion was not confined to mediæval times. Little is known of the specimen here represented, which is of silver gilt, covered externally with small pieces of mother of pearl, in the shape of feathers, applied in the manner of scales: it is supposed to be of Flemish workmanship, and has been in the collection since the year 1640.

XI.

A Jewel box or Coffer.

Height 13¼ in. Length 12¼ in.

— — · —

This beautiful coffer in ebony, one of many existing in the collection, is of Italian workmanship of the 16th century. It is richly embellished with round figures and reliefs, enamelled in the earliest manner of enamel painting, and with small plaques of gold, let into the wood with beautiful enamelled arabesques executed by the "*cloisonné*" process. It has the common form of these antique coffers, that of a small building. The roof or lid is surmounted by a recumbent figure of a boy leaning upon a skull, with an hour-glass at his feet. His head is bound with a fillet, with a medallion in front, and in his hand, he holds a book or tablet on which is to be read "memento mori". If the primary destination of this article was for the preservation of jewels, this inscription may have been intended as a warning against vanity; there is but little doubt, however, that it was originally meant for relics.

One of the cardinal or Christian virtues is represented in relief in the centre of each of the four sloping sides and ends of the lid or roof. The one visible in the plate is Charity or Christian Love. The round figures representing the theological virtues are introduced in semi-circular-headed niches upon the sides and ends of the box itself, which is of an oblong form. In the most luxurious days of ancient Rome, richly adorned jewel coffers ("Pixes") of the most elaborate workmanship were a favourite article of decoration on the toilet-tables of the Roman ladies. Their form was peculiar, generally that of a tomb or other monumental building, and at a later period after the Christian era, when they were employed as repositories for relics ("chasses"), that of a church. Similar coffers continued in use without much change of form up to the 18th century, and occur even in our times. They formed like the so-called "brides' coffers", a part of the dower, which newly married ladies of distinction brought with them to their new homes. It is well known, that in later times, many, originally intended for religious purposes, were adapted to the more mundane use, and consequently, very frequently the ornaments and allusions were singularly inappropriate and inapplicable.

XII.

Large silver-gilt Wine Cooler, or Flask.

Height 33⅞ in. Diameter of side 16¾ in.

—

This large Flask appears to have been used for cooling liquids, and it is supposed from some indications which remain, that a particular apparatus for the purpose was introduced into it. The body proper of the vessel is of a circular form, and displays on one side, in embossed work, a horseman riding at full speed, bearing before him a captive, or wounded soldier, in a singular attitude, and in the back ground a castle and encampment with soldiery. On the opposite side is represented a knight in armour standing before a captive; a castle in the act of being scaled is seen in the distance, with groups of armed men, and pieces of artillery, scattered about in front of it. Both subjects are encircled by a border of richly embossed arabesques, and surmounted by the Saxon Electoral Arms. This latter circumstance, and other reasons, have led to the supposition that these representations may refer to the taking of Gotha by the Elector Augustus.

Embossed arabesques of beautiful workmanship adorn the octangular foot, the neck, and other parts of this gigantic vessel, which, for the convenience of carriage, is provided with a handle of a somewhat singular form. The execution of the whole seems to indicate an Augsburg origin.

XIII.

Goblet of Rock Crystal, with a cover.

Height 12 in. Diameter 3½ in.

The tasteful mounting, and ornamentation, and more particularly the workmanship of the little figure on the cover of this elegant drinking vessel lead us to attribute its execution, perhaps, to the sixteenth, and certainly, at the latest, to the seventeenth century. It has been in the collection from a very early period.

XIV.

Large Ewer in Rock Crystal.

Height 9¾ in. Diameter 11 1/9 in.

Before the discovery of the art of making glass, Rock Crystal was highly prized, and much sought after for articles of luxury; not alone on account of the beauty and durability of the material, but likewise from its suitability for the arts of the stone engraver and lapidary. Vessels in this substance, filled with water, or other liquid, were placed upon the table at court banquets, and at other similar festivities. The collection of the "Green Vaults" contains more than two hundred and fifty specimens of this beautiful material, all differing in form and size, and offering a veritable mine of beautiful designs: many of them were acquired before the year 1640; and each succeeding ruler after that date added to their number.

They form an interesting chronological series; and serve to indicate epochs of taste during more than two centuries. It is clear, from several of the examples preserved here, that the original form of the stone often determined its application; either from the desire not to diminish its size, or with a view to spare labour. Lapis lazuli, precious stones, gold and silver, were lavishly expended upon mountings; and the crystal was in many cases covered with engraved designs, often of considerable artistic merit. The ewer here represented is of a spheroidal form, covered with a deeply engraved design of Italian arabesques, springing from the trunk and limbs of a grotesque Caliban-like figure, which is represented as clinging with legs and arms to the back of the vessel.

The head and shoulders of this monster are of gold enriched with enamel, and the handle and foot of the ewer are of the same material. The latter are both richly ornamented with enamelling and precious stones; and the handle especially, which is attached to the figure above described, is further remarkable for its bold graceful curve, and the grotesque masks introduced upon it. Though this specimen was not acquired till the beginning of the eighteenth century, it is evident, at the first glance, that it is the production of an earlier and better artistic period. The records of the collection attribute it to the celebrated lapidary and stone-engraver G. B. Metellino of Milan.

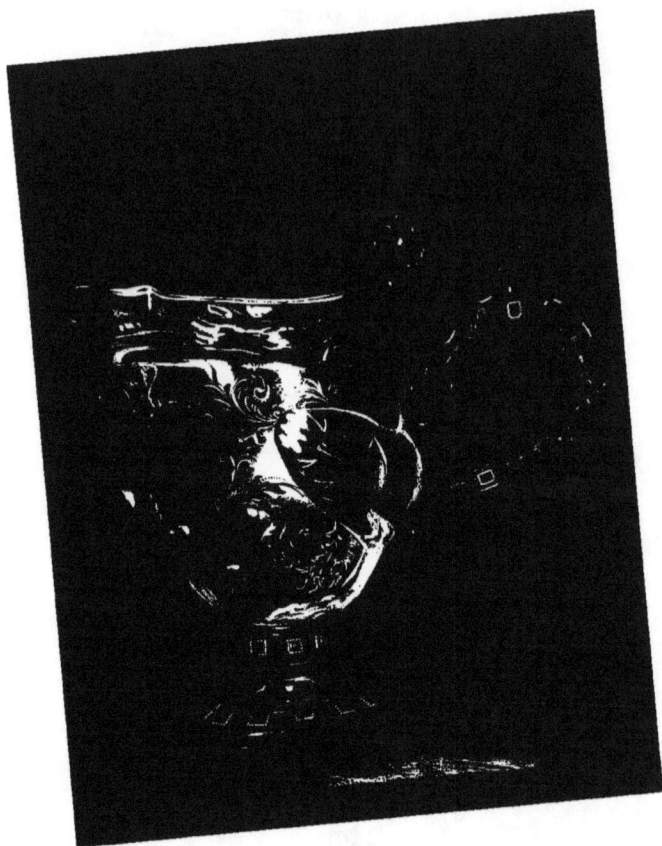

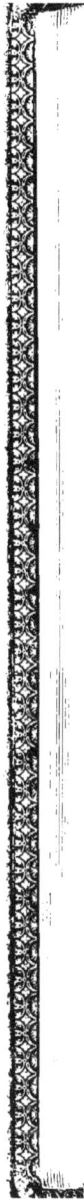

XV.

Flask or Bottle of Rock Crystal.

Height 12 in. Breadth 6¼ in.

Figures of syrens, beautifully worked in gold, and enriched with enamel and precious stones, form the handles of this magnificent bottle, which is here represented on a scale but little smaller than the original. The foot, or base, is likewise of gold, and ornamented in the the same manner as the handles. The engraved subjects on the flask itself, referring to the cultivation of the vine, are executed in somewhat shallow intaglio. The mounting and workmanship of the whole lead to the conclusion, that it was executed during the seventeenth century.

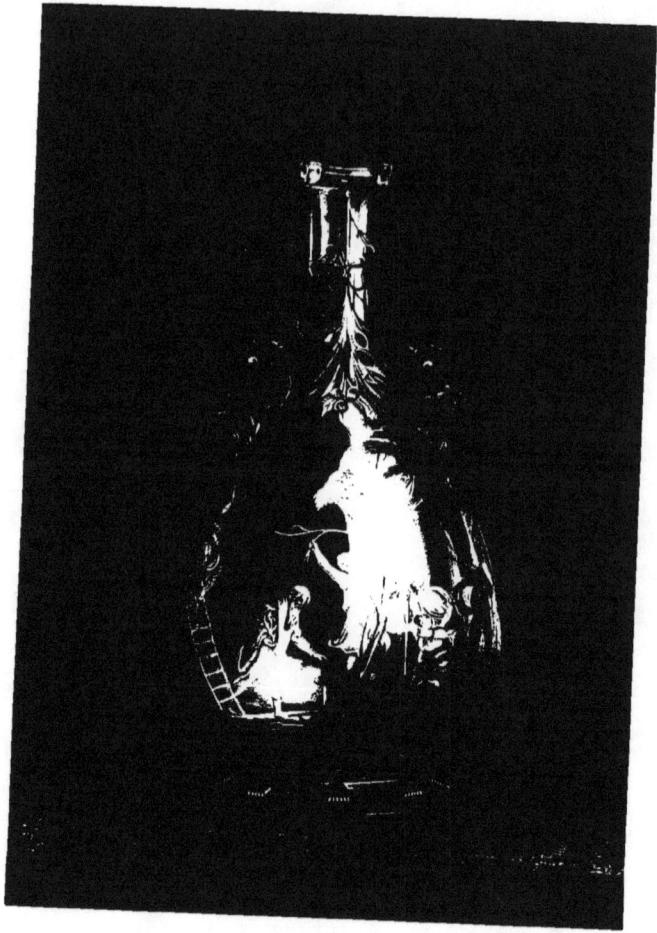

XVI.

Cup in Rock Crystal, in the shape of a Shell.

Height 18¼ in. Diameter 11½ in.

This imposing and valuable specimen, which is of original design, represents a dolphin, bearing on its head a scalloped flat cup in the shape of a shell, with its tail in the air so as to form a sort of handle to the vessel. The ornaments engraved upon the cup are insignificant. The foot, which is of an hexagonal form, is in gilt filagree work set with lapis lazuli.

XVII.

Oval scalloped Tazza of Serpentine.

Height 7⅛ in. Breadth (at the broadest part) 7¹⁄₂ in.

This magnificent specimen of oriental serpentine, mounted somewhat in the form of a lamp, is so smoothly polished that it has the effect of being almost transparent. It is partially surrounded by a gallery of silver-gilt foliated work, rising in the centre, so as to form a sort of handle of the same leafy design. Beneath this handle is represented a blue enamelled lion rampant, with a collar of diamonds, under an arch of rubies; and on either side of it, along the gallery, *five* lions in gold or blue enamel (the Danish-Norwegian arms) are introduced. On the outside of the handle are seen several small grotesque animals in enamel enriched with precious stones, and on its curved extremity is placed a model richly set of a crown, upon the head piece of which, as upon a medallion, the cipher *M. S.* and the date 1651 are to be found. This cipher is supposed to be that of Maria Sybilla, daughter of the Elector John George of Saxony, and Maria Sybilla of Brandenburgh. She married Christian V. of Denmark. and died in 1668.

XVIII.

A. Two small Vessels of dark green Jasper.

B. Small Vase of Chalcedony supporting a watch.

C. Essence or Balsam Vase of Onyx.

Height 3¼ in.

The larger of the two specimens in green jasper is mounted in silver gilt, with a flat handle terminating in a ram's head, and bears round the margin the following inscription: "Vas ex jaspide antiquum Alexandriae Aegypti repertum tali ornamento dignum." Silver gilt dolphins form the feet. The smaller vessel is in the form of an ewer, and similarly mounted.

The vase of chalcedony is from the hand of Melchior Dinglinger, and was designed as an accessory to a larger work.

The onyx essence vase is remarkable for its elegant form and tasteful ornamentation. The cover terminates in a brilliant-cut diamond.

XIX.

Ewer or Vase of Chalcedony, set with Rubies.

Height 9¼ in.

Melchior Dinglinger, the maker of this beautiful vase, evidently had an antique model in his mind, if he has not actually copied an existing object. It was intended, like another exactly similar, for an ornament of a larger piece of goldsmith's work never executed.

XX.

Portrait Statuette in ivory. The Lacemaker.

Height 4½ in. Breadth 6 in.

This statuette is selected on account of the excellence of its workmanship, its lifelike expression, and historical interest, from a collection of more than one hundred of such figures in ivory, all similarly enriched and adorned with enamel, diamonds, and other precious stones. It represents *Barbara Uttmann*, who introduced the art of lacemaking into the Saxon Erzgebirge. She was the descendant of a rich patrician family of Nuremberg, called von Elterlein, who, attracted by mining speculations, had emigrated to that mountainous region, where they settled, and made a large fortune. She was born in 1514, and was married to a rich, and much respected citizen of Annaberg, an extensive mine owner in that neighbourhood; according to the legend, she had learnt the art of lacemaking from a Flemish Protestant refugee, who had been obliged to fly from her native land to escape the persecutions of the cruel Alba, and who had found with Barbara a secure asylum. The year 1561 is assigned as the date when the latter commenced giving instruction in this art to her poorer neighbours. From Annaberg the practise of it spread over the whole Saxon Erzgebirge, and this branch of industry has proved a fruitful source of revenue up to this day to the poor inhabitants of that unproductive region: Saxon lace having been, and still being in much request as an article of luxury. Barbara died a widow in 1575 at Annaberg, leaving numerous descendants.

This statuette was executed by the jeweller Koehler of Dresden, in the beginning of the eighteenth century, whether with a commemorative object or not is unknown. At that period such expensive and richly ornamented figures were favourite articles for birthday and saintsday gifts, for Christmas and new-years presents, for mementos of family occurrences, and the like.

A. A.

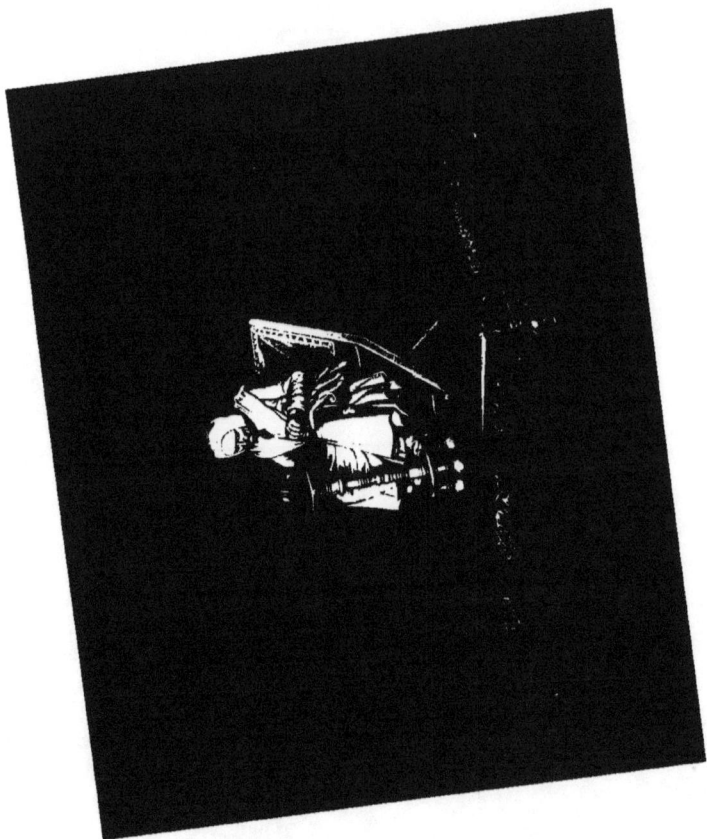

XXI.

Portrait Statuette in ivory. A Shoemaker.

Height 3¼ in.

This carefully executed statuette is the portrait of Jacob Boehme, the shoemaker and celebrated Theosoph and mystic. He was born in Silesia in 1575, of poor parents. His childhood was spent in herding cattle, and up to his tenth year he had received no instruction whatever; yet, at this early period, we find the germs of the rich forcible imagination, the devout contemplative temper and the leaning to the supernatural, which bore such abundant fruits in his later life. To this temperament, to his solitary life, and to his morbidly sensitive organization he was indebted, perhaps, for the visions and reveries, which he himself regarded as miraculous. When he was 10 years of age, with a view to qualify him for a trade, his parents sent him to school. Here he learnt to read and write, and was instructed in the fundamental principles of Christianity. The latter found a congenial soil, and struck deep root into his heart: and in the Sacred writings, more particularly in the Apocalyptical books, he found nourishment for his excitable imagination and his love of the supernatural. The trade selected for him, that of a shoemaker, gave scope for his love of contemplation, and contributed to foster it. During his apprenticeship and the years, which, in accordance with the custom of his country, he spent in travelling as a journeyman before commencing the practice of his trade as a master, he led a solitary life, given up to lonely musings upon the loftiest and most abstract subjects. The religious disputes, which were raging at that time in Saxony, excited to a certain extent his attention, but his eminently devout and Christian temper raised him above sectarian strife. The severity of his morals, and, if we may so term it, his religious consciousness contributed to increase his isolation. He was exceedingly tolerant, and neither attacked the religious opinions of others, nor was anxious to propagate his own. His extreme ignorance acted most unfavorably upon his religious, philosophical and poetical development, and, combined with his lonely dreamy life, subjected him to many delusions. In 1594 he settled at Görlitz in his native country, to practise his trade, and soon afterwards he married the daughter of a butcher, with whom he lived there for 30 years in great happiness. It would be out of place here to narrate the occurrences, in his judgement miraculous, which led him into authorship, and made him the founder of a sect of which there was a branch even in England, or to do more than allude to his supposed revelations and to his speculations, concerning God, man, nature, sin, repentance etc. etc. We find in his first writings traces of an intimate acquaintance with the Holy Scriptures, of some knowledge of a few learned authors, and of his familiarity with the speculations of the mystics and alchymists. His first work was published in 1612, his last in 1624. He was a voluminous writer, and there have been several collected, and some comparatively recent, editions of his works. For the general reader they are either unintelligible or without interest. His ideas were long considered as pure mysticism and ravings, but of later years they have excited much attention among the modern speculative philosophers of Germany. Several of his fundamental principles have been discovered to have something in common with the spirit of the philosophical systems of Spinoza, Schelling and Hegel; and he is now regarded by many as the founder of that school of philosophy. The latter years of Boehme's life were disturbed by the attacks and embittered by the enmity of the learned of that day. He bore their persecutions with the utmost sweetness and equanimity. These disputes had the effect of drawing attention to his views: he was induced by his friends to visit Dresden in 1624, and much discussion took place concerning his teachings. He was himself an object of great attention, and enjoyed the favour and esteem of the court. Soon after his return to Görlitz, he sickened and died, the 27th of November, 1624.

The artist has represented him as busily engaged at his shoe-maker's bench: the implements of his trade are of gold and enamel, and remarkably well executed. The pedestal on which the figure stands is richly ornamented with precious stones and enamel. It would seem almost as if the designer had intended a bitter irony by all this splendour, as in Boehme's face and attitude he has strikingly expressed the *malaise* and inner struggles of a man, who believes he has missed his higher and true calling, and sees himself condemned to a mechanical occupation beneath his powers. This piece is also by Koehler and of his usual excellence.

A. A.

XXII.

The Knife Grinder in ivory.

Height 3⅜ in.   Breadth 5₁₆ in.

We have already remarked in our notice of the portrait statuette of the lacemaker, that these small figures, which are so numerous in our collection, formed favourite articles for gifts. It is highly probable, that many of them were portraits of persons interesting or well known at one time. At the present day, we are in most instances unable to discover who the persons represented are, or what were the circumstances which gave them an interest, and the occasion of their acquisition and presentation remains in equal obscurity. Many of them possess a humorous character, and still excite a smile in the beholder. They are generally of creditable workmanship, the design, and modelling are good, and the expression wonderful, considering the smallness of the scale. The accessories, pedestals, etc. of them all are richly adorned with enamelling and precious stones. The specimen in our plate is from the hand of Koehler, and very characteristic of that master.

XXIII.

A. Two grotesque Figures. (Perles monstres.)

The trunks formed of large misshapen pearls
Height 5¼ in.

B. A Tazza or small round Basin with a cover.

Enamelled and decorated with arabesques
Size of the original.

A. The two figures here given are selected from a complete gallery of such productions. They may, perhaps, represent Falstaff and Punch, and were executed in the year 1705 by a Leipsic jeweller of the name of Ferbeck. The taste for these grotesque figures was at its height in the latter end of the seventeenth, and beginning of the eighteenth century, though it had its origin much earlier; we find traces of it even among the Romans. This department of the collection is extraordinarily rich. The best specimens are from the hands of the jewellers Melchior Dinglinger, Koehler and Nessler of Dresden, Gerardet of Berlin and Ferbeck of Frankfort a. M. These artists displayed great skill and ingenuity in availing themselves of the accidental forms of the large distorted pearls, which not only suggested their work, but likewise furnished its main material. Many of those here preserved are of great size, and some of the finest lustre. They formed in most instances the trunk and limbs of the figure, while diamonds, precious stones, gold, and enamel, were freely expended upon the inferior parts, and upon the accessories. The workmanship of most of them is admirable.

B. This richly enamelled Tazza or Basin, was probably intended for sugar. The style of the decoration is singular, but striking, the colours are brilliant and forcible, and the effect is rich and harmonious.

XXIV.

Drinking Vessel of Rhinoceros Horn in the shape of a Shell.

Height 15,⁸⁄₁₀ in. Breadth 5¼ in.

An enamelled gold dragon, bearing the Insignia of the Danish order of the Elephant, is placed upon the summit of the shell, which forms the cup of this richly ornamented vessel. Beneath it, behind, upon an enamelled plaque are represented Mars and Venus. The shell is borne upon the head of a statue of Diana in rhinoceros horn, which terminates below the waist in the form of a herme. On this several small enamelled medallions are to be found, and the whole is lavishly adorned with pearls, precious stones, and enamel. A mistake can hardly be made in attributing this specimen to Melchior Dinglinger, who delighted in mythological "Rococo".

XXV.

Watch and Watch-stand.

Height 9¼ in.

This costly specimen, from the hand of the jeweller Koehler of Dresden, in pure *Rococo* taste, has but little pretension to artistic beauty of form, but makes a very pleasing impression, notwithstanding, from the judicious application of enamelling, and the tasteful arrangement of the precious stones, with which it is richly set. The foot is particularly worthy of attention. The watch itself was made by Droynot of Poitiers.

XXVI.

Reliquary of Rock Crystal.

Height 5¾ in. Breadth 3¾ in.

The form and ornaments of this oblong coffret leave no doubt that it was intended for the preservation of relics. In the sides and ends are introduced four plaques of rock crystal, on which are engraved, with extreme delicacy, scenes from the Passion. The cover, which slopes towards the top like a roof, consists of four similar plaques, on which are represented, in similar style, the Maries, and the Resurrection and Ascension of our Lord. The coffret, which is further adorned with enamelled designs, into which are introduced the implements of the Passion etc. etc., has four small pillars at the angles, surmounted by beautifully enamelled figures of the Evangelists, with their attributes. This reliquary was made in Breslau by Daniel Voght, a native of Bohemia settled in that city.

XXVII.

Two Pendant Jewels, Orders, or Decorations.

Pendant Jewels, under different names, were formerly very much in use as marks of favour from Princes, as memorials of weddings, contracts, birth-days, and the like, as prizes at tournaments, and for many other purposes; and may be regarded as contributions to the family and private history of reigning houses. They were worn suspended from magnificent neck chains, or collars of gold, usually presented with them; and upon the death of the receiver were, in many instances, deposited in the family treasury for preservation. It is not difficult to guess the occurrence commemorated by the first example in our plate, where Paris is depicted bestowing the golden apple upon the most beautiful of the Goddesses. It was most probably conferred upon a lady at her betrothal.

These decorations or "faveurs" were generally of beautiful and artistic workmanship, and bore always some reference to the occasion of their foundation and presentation, by means of delicate allegories in the subjects represented, by initial letters in precious stones, mottoes, or other devices.

XXVIII.

Vase of Agate superbly mounted in Gold and Enamel, and richly ornamented with Precious Stones.

Height 16⅜ in.   Breadth 4 ⁷⁄₉ in.   Length 12 in.

This costly specimen of the goldsmith's and enameller's art is the work of the celebrated Melchior Dinglinger, and displays perfectly the characteristics of his manner, namely, extreme magnificence of general effect, united with great elegance in the details. It has the general form of a lamp, and represents the bath of Diana. The handle is formed by an undraped figure of that goddess, carved in ivory, with one arm upraised as if warding off something. She sits at one end of the oval agate vessel, which represents the bowl of the lamp, and which is mounted as a bath, beneath a fantastically adorned canopy; at the other end, above the burner, which is partially covered with a piece of drapery, is placed her favourite dog, keeping watch over her implements of the chase. Along the margin of the vessel, upon brackets, are to be seen several small articles for the use of the bath; and on its outer surface, beneath the figures of Diana and the dog, the portraits of a couple of the fair favourites of Augustus the Strong, the Countess Cosel, and the beautiful Aurora von Königsmark, are introduced, painted in enamel. Our plate affords but a glimpse of that of the last named lady, much foreshortened. The whole rests upon the extreme points of the antlers of a stag, which is represented as being torn in pieces by dogs, and forms the foot of the lamp.

It is clear that this design is intended as an allusion to the fate of Actaeon, from the inscription in small diamonds, "Effronterie perd—Discrétion sert", which surrounds the circular base upon which it is placed.

How highly this work was esteemed by Dinglinger himself is apparent from his having had it introduced into his portrait by his friend Antoine Pesne. An engraving after this picture forms the vignette on the title-page of this work. A short notice of this distinguished man, the best part of whose life was spent in the service of the Saxon court, and whose principal works are preserved in the "Green Vaults" in Dresden, will not be misplaced here, as from these circumstances his reputation has been more confined and local than his great merits deserve. He was born at Biberich, near Ulm, in the year 1665. Nobody who is acquainted with his productions will deny that he was gifted by nature with the artistic sense, however much its manifestation may have been influenced and obscured by the accidents of his position, and the requirements and taste of his time. The vicinity of his birthplace to Augsburg, then the great seat of the goldsmith's art, probably determined his choice of a profession; though the devotion with which he pursued it during his whole life, would seem to indicate a passionate natural inclination, fortunately not opposed by circumstances. It is clear, from his works themselves, that he enjoyed a careful and liberal education in addition to the professional training, which he received at Augsburg, and which he subsequently perfected, by repeated journeys in Italy and France. Early in life he attracted the attention of Augustus the Strong, Elector of Saxony, and King of Poland, of whose love of splendour and art our collection possesses so many proofs. By him Dinglinger was induced in the year 1702 to settle in Dresden, where he spent the remainder of his life. His house, which was fitted up with great originality, soon became a centre of attraction to artists, and to eminent men in all departments of knowledge, from the geniality and kindly humour of its good-natured owner. No distinguished traveller left Dresden without visiting his workshop. The Czar Peter the Great of Russia is said to have been his guest when he passed through that city; and his royal employer was his frequent visitor, and was fond of watching him at his work. He was indebted to that monarch for many suggestions, and he discussed with him the plan of many of the works which he afterwards executed. From the sketches and estimates made for his productions, which, with the receipts and all other documents concerning them, are preserved in the archives of the "Green Vaults", we gather that they were all undertaken at his own expense, and carried out from his own means, or credit. If we consider their number, and their costly nature, we are astonished at the material resources of the man; if we think of their variety, and the extraordinary labour, and perseverance which their execution required, we are lost in admiration of his inventive faculties, and moral qualities. The explanation is to be found in the high character of the artist, and in his genuine love of his art, to which he devoted himself, without wasting his time, and the powers of his mind, on the external world, and its transient interests. He seems to have laboured, with a sincere love of his work, for fame alone, without a thought of gain or wealth. The number and magnitude of some of the productions which issued from his workshop, most of which are to be seen in the "Green Vaults", are, besides, partly to be accounted for by the assistance which he received from his brothers, and other members of his family, whom he summoned to Dresden when his reputation was established; one of the former was a very clever painter in enamel, of whose skill the collection in Dresden presents many valuable examples; the other was a mere ordinary working jeweller. John Melchior Dinglinger, the subject of our notice, died in Dresden, in 1731, leaving one son, also a goldsmith. Several of his father's unfinished works were completed by him.